Sew Mini TREATS

More Than 18 Food Plushies to Stitch & Stuff

by the editors of Klutz

KLUTZ®

CONTENTS

What YOU GET

8 colors of embroidery floss

9 colors of felt

Stuffing

strawberry

bacon

leaf 2

apple

doughnut

toast

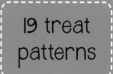
19 treat patterns

2 embroidery needles with holder

30 pre-cut eyes and 30 pre-cut cheeks

Other stuff you'll need:
scissors
(small, sharp blades to cut felt)

Optional:
ribbon, ruler, thimble, pen

START
HERE

Learn the basic skills you'll need to sew all of your treats by completing the doughnut before you move on.

DOUGHNUT

Not only are these doughnuts adorable, they're a great way to start your training as a Mini Treats sewing chef!

Almost every project will use a needle, a small handful of stuffing, and scissors, so keep those handy. For the patterns, floss, and felt you need, check the recipe card. Here's what you'll need for the doughnut:

Recipe

INGREDIENTS:
- Tan floss
- Pink floss
- Other floss colors for sprinkles

TRACE AND CUT:

x2

2 doughnut pieces   I doughnut frosting

TRACING

You'll find patterns in the box that will help you make all of the treats in this book.

1 Take the doughnut pattern and place it on top of a piece of tan felt. Lay it very close to the edges to get the most out of the felt without wasting too much. (See the pattern guide in the box.)

2 Take a pen and trace around the pattern, on the outside and inside.

3 Place the doughnut pattern on the tan felt again, very close to the first one you traced. Trace the inside and outside of the pattern again.

Now you're ready to trace and cut the frosting in the same way! (You only need one frosting.)

You can set the patterns aside for now.

CUTTING

1 Using sharp scissors, very carefully cut along the lines you've drawn on the outside of your shapes. When you're done, one side might have lines or marks from tracing on it. That's now called the "wrong side" of the felt. Wrong sides always end up on the inside of the finished treat, so you won't see them.

2 To cut out the center holes: Fold the trimmed circle in half (with the lines on the outside) and snip a small cut into the fold. Be sure not to cut past your lines on either side.

3 Now, unfold the circle and insert your scissors into the cut. Snip gently until you reach the line you traced, and then cut along it.

4 Repeat Steps 1–3 for the second doughnut piece and again for the frosting. They should all have holes of similar size at their centers.

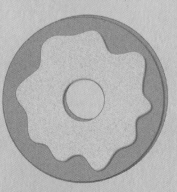

USING FLOSS

Embroidery floss usually has six separate strands wound together. For the projects in this book, you'll only need two strands at a time. Here's how to separate them.

1 Take the bundle of floss you want to use, remove the rubber band, and unwind about 14 inches (35.5 cm). Cut it off.

2 Take the cut floss and hold it gently in one hand, about 1 inch (2.5 cm) from the end.

3 With your other hand, pull one strand of floss up . . .

. . . and away from the other strands.

4 You now have one strand of floss ready to go. Repeat Steps 2–3 one more time.

5 Take your two separated strands of floss, smooth them out and line them up together.

Fresh
TIPS
Keep spare strands of floss loose and untangled, so you can use them later for another project.

Threading
THE NEEDLE

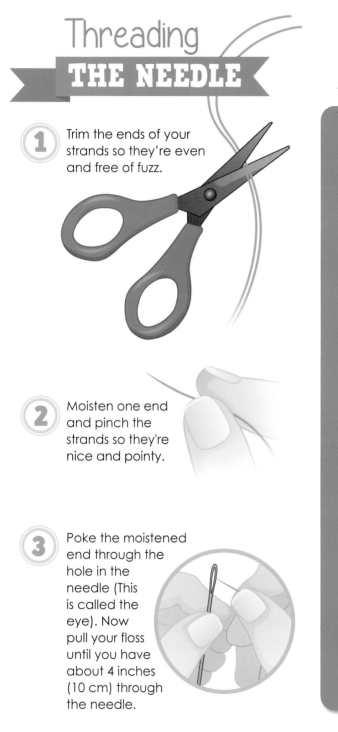

1 Trim the ends of your strands so they're even and free of fuzz.

2 Moisten one end and pinch the strands so they're nice and pointy.

3 Poke the moistened end through the hole in the needle (This is called the eye). Now pull your floss until you have about 4 inches (10 cm) through the needle.

SAFETY STUFF

- Always handle needles with care. Don't rush the stitches.

- Needles are sharp. If you have a thimble, wear it to protect your fingertips while stitching.

- Keep needles away from small children, pets, and bare feet.

- Store your needles when you're finished working. You can use the needle holder provided, or a storage unit of your choice.

- If a needle breaks, carefully check the surrounding area and throw out broken needle pieces.

- If a needle breaks the skin, gently clean the area and apply a bandage. Get an adult to help you.

- These treats are for decoration only. Do not give them to small children to play with.

- If finished projects get dirty, spot-clean them with a damp rag and warm water. Do not wash the felt in a washing machine.

- Supplies included should only be used with felt.

Tying a
STARTING KNOT

1 Hold the threaded needle in your right hand. With your left, pick up the long end of your floss. Place the end of the floss behind the needle and flat against it, close to the tip.

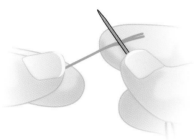

2 Holding the needle and floss gently in place with your right index finger, use your left hand to wrap the floss around the needle three or four times.

3 Move your right thumb up to hold the new wraps of floss in place, then let go of the floss with your left hand.

4 Carefully grab the middle of the needle with your left hand and use your right to pull the wrapped floss down over the eye of the needle and all the way to the end of the floss. It should tie a knot right near the end of your strands.

ADDING FACES

Making the eyes first helps you line up the rest of the face.

Eyes &

CHEEKS

 1 Place eyes on the frosting about ¼ inch (0.6 cm) from the center hole.

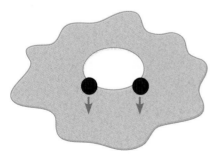

2 Using a needle threaded with black floss, poke up through the back of your felt and through the eye.

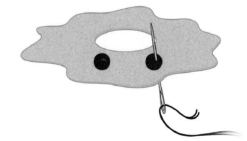

Attach the cheeks in the same way you added the eyes, with one small stitch in pink floss.

For winking eyes, stitch a small sideways "V" using a back stitch (page 14).

Eyelashes can be added to fancy things up.

 Poke your needle back through the other side of the eye and finish your floss (page 17). Repeat Steps 1–2 to attach the second eye.

 Use white floss to make two small stitches in the middle of each eye for maximum cuteness.

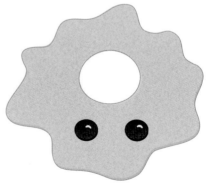

ADDING A MOUTH

Back Stitch

With a smile or a frown, making a mouth is the final step to the cute food face.

1 Poke your needle up through the bottom of the felt and pull floss until the starting knot just touches the felt. Now poke your needle back through the felt to make one very small stitch.

2 Poke your needle up through the bottom again, one stitch length away from your first stitch.

3 Now you'll do something a little different: Poke your needle into the ending hole of your last stitch and then poke it back out one stitch length past your starting point.

4 Pull your floss all the way through until it lies flat without puckering. That's one back stitch!

5 Continue repeating Steps 3–4 until you reach the end of the mouth. Poke back through the felt one more time, so you are at the back of the felt, then finish your floss (page 17).

Adding
SPRINKLES

Little stitches make great sprinkles. Try using three or four colors to make your doughnut darling.

1 With your first color, make a few stitches at random around the frosting. Each stitch should be about $1/8$ of an inch long (0.3 cm). Finish your floss (page 17).

2 Repeat Step 1 with your other colors.

Fresh
TIPS
Try not to cross the hole of the doughnut with floss.

Finishing
FLOSS

1 Turn the felt over so that you're looking at the wrong side. Poke the needle under one of the nearby stitches (not through the felt) to create a loop.

2 Wrap the end of the floss around your needle two or three times.

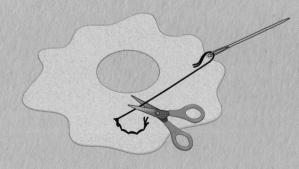

3 Pull the needle until a knot forms near your felt. Cut your floss close to the knot. Your floss is now secure!

If you find this too hard, or if your floss just isn't long enough, you can try this other method for finishing your floss:

- Take the needle off of your two strands of floss.
- Separate the strands and tie a knot with them.
- Do this a couple of times, then cut the floss close to the knot.

You've got your frosting looking great with a cute little face and plenty of pretty sprinkles. Now it's time to assemble the doughnut.

Attaching
THE FROSTING

Whip Stitch

1 Thread your needle with two strands of pink floss (page 10). Lay the frosting face up onto the "good" side of one doughnut piece. Make sure the holes of the two pieces line up.

2 Poke your needle through the back of the doughnut piece just outside the edge of the frosting. Pull the floss all the way through.

3 Poke your needle back down about $1/8$ inch (0.3 cm), straight across the frosting edge. Pull the needle through to make one whip stitch.

4 Keep on stitching this way until you come back around to the place you started. Finish your floss.

Attaching
THE CENTER

1 Thread your needle with two strands of pink floss, then poke your needle through the back of the frosted doughnut piece about ¹/₈ inch (0.3 cm) away from the edge of the center hole. Pull it all the way through. The knot should be on the wrong side of the felt.

2 Take the frosted and unfrosted doughnut pieces and lay them together so that the "wrong" sides are facing on the inside of the doughnut. (See page 8 for a reminder about "wrong" sides)

3 Bring your floss around and poke your needle through the bottom layer and back through to the front.

Starting knot is here.

4 Keep repeating Step 3 until you are back at the starting point. Finish your floss on one of the stitches you've made.

Stuffing
& FINISHING

Now that the center of your doughnut is all connected, it's time to have some fun and add the stuffing. Take the stuffing out of the bag and pull it apart so it's nice and fluffy.

 1 Using two strands of tan floss, stitch the outside edges of your doughnut sides. Stop after 1 inch (2.5 cm).

 2 Take a small pinch (a little goes a long way) of the stuffing and push it into the area of the doughnut you've just sewn. It's easier if you roll the stuffing in your fingers first.

 3 Repeat Steps 1–2, sewing and stuffing until you reach about 1 inch away from where you started. This is your chance to adjust the stuffing. Try using the eraser end of a pencil to make it spread out evenly.

4 Once your doughnut is nice and fluffy, go ahead and make those last few stitches to close it up, then finish your floss.

If you need more stuffing, try using cotton balls or scrap felt pieces.

You've DONE A DOUGHNUT!

Fresh
TIPS

Finish your floss on stitches near the back of your treats so the knots won't show from the front.

Custom made with love!

SWEETS

Sprinkles, nuts, hearts, and, of course, faces are just some of the options you can choose. Now that you're a master doughnut maker, try a second doughnut of your own design.

TOASTER PASTRY

Recipe

INGREDIENTS:
- Tan floss
- Pink floss
- Other floss colors (for sprinkles)

TRACE AND CUT:

x2

2 toaster pastry pieces

1 toaster pastry frosting

DECORATE

1 Add a face and sprinkles to the frosting (page 12) for maximum sweetness.

ASSEMBLE

2 Lay your frosting face up on one toaster pastry piece. Attach it using whip stitch (page 18).

3 Attach the two sides together (wrong sides facing). Stop 1 inch (2.5 cm) before the end so you can stuff the pastry.

Toasty!

4 Once you've got it stuffed just enough (not too much), continue stitching to close the gap, then finish your floss.

CHOCOLATE CHIP COOKIE

DECORATE

 1 Add a face to the cookie (page 12) and lay out your dark brown chips to see if you like the arrangement.

 2 Once you do, use black floss to make to make small x's in each chip. Attach some more chips on the other cookie piece as well if you'd like.

ASSEMBLE

3 Attach the two cookie sides together (wrong sides facing). Stop 1 inch (2.5 cm) before the end so you can stuff it . . .

. . . then finish the seam.

Recipe

INGREDIENTS:
- Tan floss
- Black floss

TRACE AND CUT:

2 cookie pieces   6-10 chocolate chips

Chip chip hooray!

EGG

Over easy!

Recipe

INGREDIENTS:
- White floss
- Yellow floss

TRACE AND CUT:

x2

2 egg whites   1 egg yolk

DECORATE

1 Add a face to the egg yolk (page 12).

ASSEMBLE

2 Attach the yolk to the right side of one egg white using yellow floss. Stop about halfway and add a tiny bit of stuffing before you finish.

3 Attach the two egg whites (wrong sides facing). Stop 1 inch (2.5 cm) before the end so you can stuff it, then continue stitching to close the seam.

Fresh TIPS

If you have an irregularly shaped pattern with top and bottom pieces, try this: Trace the top with the pattern face up, and the bottom with the pattern face down. This will keep all of your pen marks hidden on the inside.

BACON

Recipe

INGREDIENTS:
- Red floss
- White floss

TRACE AND CUT:

x2

x4

2 bacon pieces

4 bacon stripes

DECORATE

 1 Stitch the stripes onto one bacon piece using small stitches down the middle. You can cut and bend the stripes to fit any way you want. Repeat for the other side.

 2 Add a face to the front of the bacon—pick a place where it shows well (page 12).

ASSEMBLE

 3 Attach the two bacon sides together (wrong sides facing). Stop 1 inch (2.5 cm) before the end so you can add stuffing.

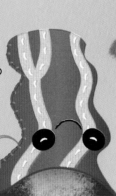

Continue stitching to close the seam.

Love this bacon to bits!

Small BITES

These tiny treats don't need much stuffing to be sweet.

LIME

DECORATE

① Add a sewn face (page 12) to one side of your lime.

ASSEMBLE

② Attach the two lime pieces together like you did for the doughnut (page 20), stuff, and then close.

You can add tiny details with stitches.

Recipe

INGREDIENTS:
- Green floss
- Ribbon (optional)

TRACE AND CUT:

x2

2 lime pieces

If you want to add a ribbon, see page 29.

ORANGE

Recipe

INGREDIENTS:
- Orange floss
- Green floss
- Ribbon (optional)

TRACE AND CUT:

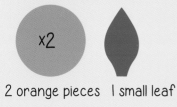

x2

2 orange pieces   1 small leaf

DECORATE

① Add a sewn face (page 12) to one side of your orange and sew the leaf above it.

ASSEMBLE

② Attach the two orange pieces together, stuff, then close.

ICE CREAM CONE

Recipe

INGREDIENTS:
- Black floss
- Tan floss
- Pink floss
- Ribbon (optional)

TRACE AND CUT:

2 ice cream scoops — x2

2 ice cream cones — x2

2 topping pieces — x2

Fresh
TIPS
To make a sugar cone, you can add a grid of stitches in a diamond pattern. Just keep your stitches small and your lines close together.

DECORATE

1 Add a sewn face (page 12) to one side of your ice cream scoop.

ASSEMBLE

2 Attach the topping, scoop and cone pieces together. Use black floss for the topping.

3 Attach the two finished sides together, changing floss colors for each section—then stuff and finish.

PINEAPPLE

DECORATE

1 Add a diamond pattern of stitches in tan floss, then sew a face (page 12) onto one side of your pineapple.

ASSEMBLE

2 Using yellow floss, attach the two pineapple sides together. Leave room at the top for the leaf, then stuff.

ADD A RIBBON LOOP

Fold a ribbon in half and insert the ends into a gap in the seam before you finish stitching. Attach the ribbon with a few straight stitches, then finish your floss on a whip stitch.

Recipe

INGREDIENTS:
- Yellow floss
- Green floss
- Ribbon (optional)

TRACE AND CUT:

x2

2 pineapple pieces   1 pineapple leaf

3 To attach the leaf, put it between the two yellow pineapple sides and make a few small straight stitches that go through both yellow sides and the leaf. Finish your floss when the pineapple is completely closed.

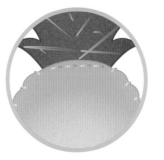

Stuffed SNACKS

Puffy and fluffy, these treats are too sweet to eat.

LEMON

Recipe

INGREDIENTS:
- Yellow floss
- Green floss

TRACE AND CUT:

x4

4 lemon pieces

1 lemon leaf

1 lemon stem

DECORATE

1 Add a face to one piece of the lemon (page 12). Place it close to the center where there is more room.

ASSEMBLE

2 Line up the piece with a sewn face and one blank piece so the right sides are facing. (The sewn face will be on the inside.)

3 With yellow floss, attach the two pieces together along one side, but don't go all the way to the top. Finish your floss.

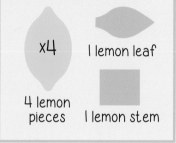

4 Take a third lemon piece and line it up with the edge of one of the already-sewn pieces, then use the whip stitch to attach one side of these pieces together. Finish your floss.

5 For the last piece, attach one side to an already-sewn piece and finish; then attach the other side to your first piece in the same way you did the others.

6 Now turn the lemon right-side out. You can use the end of a pencil to push out tough corners and edges.

7 Stuff your lemon until it's just full, but don't over-stuff it.

ATTACHING THE LEAF

8 Roll up the stem and stitch it into a tube with two strands of green floss.

9 Attach the stem to the top of the lemon by poking your needle through the top of the back of the lemon, through the stem, and through the lemon top at the front. Then, poke your needle back through all three layers again so that you have a small stitch at the front holding the stem in place.

10 Stitch the lemon leaf to the stem, near the base.

11 Use yellow floss to stitch up the top of the lemon around the stem on all four seams.

Fresh
TIPS
For fancier (and sturdier) leaves, you can stitch down the middle and sides before you attach them. Try a few patterns on the leaves in other projects for fun.

APPLE

Recipe

INGREDIENTS:
- Red floss
- Green floss
- Black floss

TRACE AND CUT:

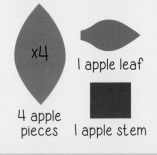

x4

4 apple pieces

1 apple leaf

1 apple stem

DECORATE

1 Add a face to one piece of the apple (page 12). Place it close to the center to make sure it will show.

ASSEMBLE

2 Using red floss, attach the four sides just like you did for the lemon, then turn it right side out and stuff until it's just full (pages 31–32).

ATTACHING THE LEAF

3 Roll up the stem and stitch it together with black floss, then attach it as you did for the lemon (page 33).

4 Using green floss, stitch the leaf to the apple near the base of the stem, then close up the top seams of the apple with red floss.

FINISHING

5 Thread your needle with red floss and make an extra-big starting knot.

6 Squeeze the top and bottom of the apple together so that they almost touch, then poke your needle through the top of the apple and down through the bottom. The knot should be on the top still.

7 Keeping the top and bottom pinched in, finish your floss at the bottom of the apple. Now you should have an indent at each end that gives it an apple shape.

Teacher's pet!

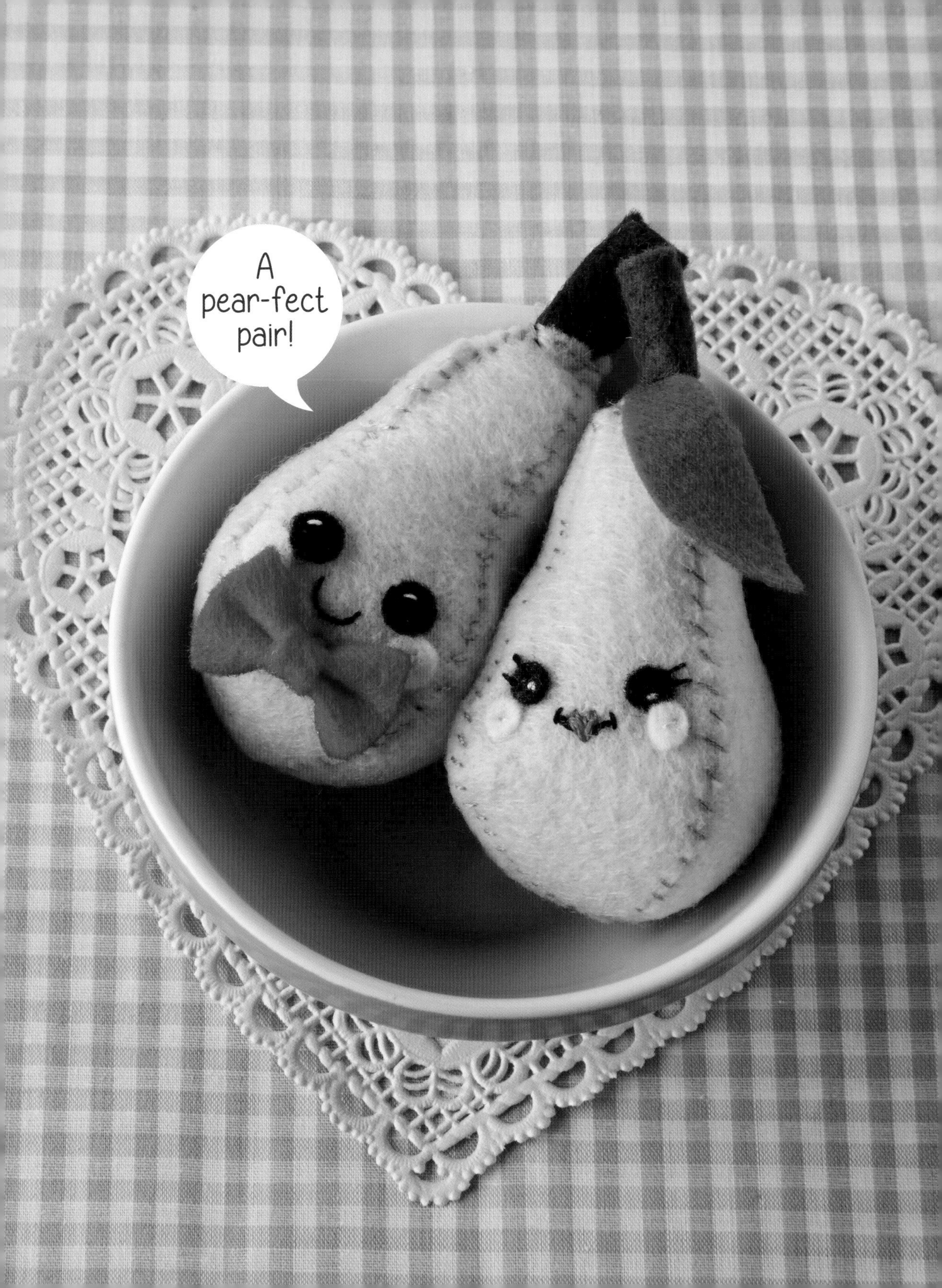
A pear-fect pair!

PEAR

DECORATE

1 Add a face to one piece of the pear (page 12). Place it close to the center to make sure it will show.

ASSEMBLE

2 Using green floss, attach the four sides one at a time just like you did for the lemon (page 31), then turn it right side out and stuff until it's just full.

Recipe

INGREDIENTS:
- Green floss
- Black floss

TRACE AND CUT:

x4

4 pear pieces

1 pear leaf

1 pear stem

ATTACHING THE STEM & LEAF

3 Roll up the dark brown felt and sew it closed with black floss. Then attach it to your pear leaf using green floss.

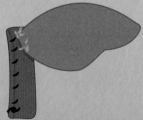

4 Use green floss to attach the stem and finish up the four seams at the top.

CUPCAKE

Recipe

INGREDIENTS:
- Tan floss
- Black floss
- Optional: other colors of floss for sprinkles (page 6)

TRACE AND CUT:

1 cupcake frosting

1 cupcake bottom

1 cupcake top

1 cupcake base

DECORATE

1 Add a face on the cupcake base (page 12).

ASSEMBLE

2 With tan floss, attach the cupcake base to the cupcake bottom.

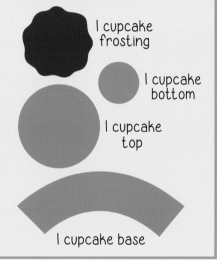

3 Now attach the two sides of the base together. It's OK if the bottom is a little rippled, it won't show.

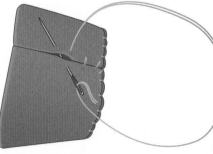

4 Stuff the base of the cupcake lightly and set it aside.

5 Decorate the frosting with sprinkles if you want them (page 16), and attach it to the cupcake top (page 18).

6 It's time to attach the cupcake top to the liner. Start with four stitches spaced around the front, back, and both sides. Finish the floss after each. This will help your top stay even.

I'm stuffed.

7 Now add just a bit more stuffing to make the top nice and puffy, and sew the stitches in between your four anchor points.

Fresh
TIPS

Cut a small circle of red felt, about 2 inches (5 cm). Gather it to make a small cherry (see page 47 for how to gather).

Side ORDERS

TOAST

Recipe

INGREDIENTS:
• Tan floss

TRACE AND CUT:

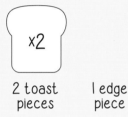

x2

2 toast pieces | 1 edge piece

DECORATE

 1 Add a face on the white part of one toast piece (page 12).

ADD THE EDGE

2 Lay the edge piece against one of your toast pieces, wrong sides together. Pull the starting knot through the tan fabric between the sides so it won't show.

Fresh
TIPS
If you'd like to customize your toast, use leftover pieces of red felt to make jelly, or add a small square of yellow butter.

3 With tan floss, use whip stitch to completely attach your edge piece all the way around the toast.

4 If you have a little extra crust, trim it and then sew the edges together with a couple of stitches.

5 Take your other toast piece and stitch it to the other edge of your crust. Be sure the wrong side is facing inside.

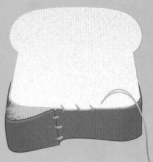

6 Continue stitching around the toast until you have about a 1 inch (2.5 cm) opening. Stuff the toast until it's just full, but don't over-stuff it. Continue stitching to close the gap.

I'm the toast of the town!

POPSICLE

One cool dude!

Recipe

INGREDIENTS:
- Orange floss
- Black floss

TRACE AND CUT:

x2

2 Popsicle pieces

I edge piece

I stick

I cream filling

DECORATE

1 Make a face on one of the orange sides of the Popsicle (page 12).

ASSEMBLE

2 Using orange floss, attach the orange edge to the back of one Popsicle piece (see the toast instructions on page 41).

3 Fold the brown felt in half and then stitch it together along the side. Trim the bottom into a rounded shape if you'd like.

4 Attach the stick to the bottom of the Popsicle with orange floss. Let it stick out about 2 inches (5 cm).

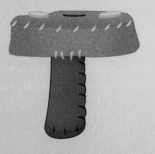

5 Attach the Popsicle piece, sewing right over the stick as you go. Leave a small opening, stuff, and close.

Fresh TIPS

For a cute cream filling, use a tiny snippet of white felt in the bite mark. Attach it with orange floss.

WATERMELON

Recipe

INGREDIENTS:
- White floss
- Red floss
- Black floss
  (for the seeds)

TRACE AND CUT:

2 fruit pieces

x2

x2

I skin piece

2 rind pieces

I side piece

DECORATE

1 Make a face on one red side of the fruit (page 12).

2 Add seeds by stitching black teardrop shapes, or make your watermelon seedless.

ASSEMBLE

3 Attach a red fruit piece to a rind piece using red floss.

Repeat for the other fruit and rind pieces.

4 Attach the skin to the back of one of the white rinds using white floss. Trim the green felt if needed.

5 Using red floss, attach the watermelon side piece to the green skin and one fruit/rind combo.

6 Still using red floss, attach the other fruit/rind piece to the red side piece.

7 Stuff the watermelon and sew that last seam closed with white floss.

Summer sweet!

PIZZA

Recipe

INGREDIENTS:
- White floss
- Red floss
- Tan floss

TRACE AND CUT:

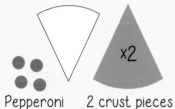

I cheese piece

Pepperoni

 x2

2 crust pieces

I back piece

I side piece

DECORATE

1 Make a face on the white cheese (page 12).

2 Cut some red felt into circles to make pepperoni (or tomatoes) and attach them.

3 Attach the white cheese piece to one of the crust pieces. Make sure the points at the bottom line up.

4 Use tan floss to attach the side piece, back piece, and final crust (see the watermelon instructions on page 44).

Upper crust!

45

Recipe

INGREDIENTS:
- Orange floss
- Green floss
- Yellow floss (optional)

TRACE AND CUT:

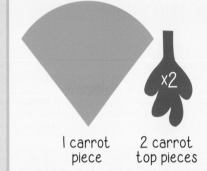

| I carrot piece | 2 carrot top pieces |

CARROT

DECORATE

1 Make a face on one side of the carrot (page 12).

ASSEMBLE

2 Fold the carrot piece in half so the wrong side is facing out.

3 Stitch the straight edges together using orange floss. Finish the floss.

4 Turn the carrot right side out by pushing the pointy end through the top.

5 With orange floss, poke your needle into the top of the carrot, about ½ inch (1 cm) away from the edge. Pull the floss through until the knot hits the felt gently.

 6 Keeping the distance from the top about the same, make large, loose stitches all the way around the top. Be sure your last stitch finishes on the inside of the carrot. Remove the needle.

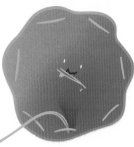

 7 Stuff the carrot to just below your stitched line. Gently use a pencil to stuff the very tip of the carrot if it's hard to reach.

Thanks a bunch!

 8 Arrange your two carrot tops the way you want them to look, then stitch them (with orange floss) into one side of your carrot. Be sure you attach them below your loose sewn line. Finish the floss.

9 Now take the loose floss at the top of your carrot and pull it closed like a drawstring. This is called gathering.

 10 Make a few more stitches to keep the carrot closed, and finish your floss near the gathered seam.

STRAWBERRY

Recipe

INGREDIENTS:
• Red floss
• Green floss

TRACE AND CUT:
1 strawberry

1 strawberry leaf

The strawberry is made just like the carrot. Use red felt and sew a green four-corner leaf on top for a cute little berry.